Made in the USA
Coppell, TX
05 January 2023

10471662R00057